BRASS IN COLOR

Beginner Method Series

TRUMPET

LESSON BOOK TWO

by Sean Burdette

Illustrations by
David Orr, BLUE ASTER STUDIO
Bloomington, IN

ISBN 13: 978-1-7320252-1-9
Copyright © 2018 BRASS IN COLOR, LLC
All Rights Reserved.

Any duplication, adaptation or arrangement of the compositions, tablature design and illustrations contained in this collection and series requires the written consent of the publisher. Unauthorized uses are an infringement of the U.S. Copyright Act and are punishable by law.

Introduction

Trumpet Book Two of the Brass in Color Beginner Method Series uses a color-coded tablature (Color Fingerings) to help students learn the fingerings of the trumpet and apply them to notes in the Low Range.

The Low Range begins with the note **C** notated below the staff, and the remaining notes of the Low Range are presented in a descending chromatic order and end with the notes **G♭/F♯** that are also notated below the staff. For each lesson the notes of the Low Range will be introduced relative to the notes of the Middle Range, and these notes will correspond with the Color Fingerings. In this way students will be able to see how the same fingerings are used to play different notes on the trumpet.

In addition to learning the notes of the Low Range, students will be introduced to the music concepts of slurs, eighth notes and scales.

Standard music notation has also been included with each lesson to help the instructor know which notes to play, and to teach students how to read the notes as they match them with the fingerings of the trumpet. Breath marks, articulation, dynamics and tempi are not noted in the lessons and may be added by the instructor as needed. Also, key signatures are not used so that students will focus primarily on listening and learning the fingerings associated with the notes.

This beginner method series for trumpet also has a companion website:

BRASS IN COLOR (www.brassincolor.com)

On the website you will find audio for each lesson as well as different activities, videos and other resources to help students learn to play the trumpet.

Contents

Lesson 1	4
Lesson 2	6
Technique Exercises 1	8
Songs Group 1	10
Songs Group 2	12
Lesson 3	14
Lesson 4	16
Technique Exercises 2	18
Technique Exercises 3	20
Songs Group 3	22
Songs Group 4	24
Songs Group 5	26
Lesson 5	28
Lesson 6	30
Lesson 7	32
Technique Exercises 4	34
Technique Exercises 5	36
Songs Group 6	38
Songs Group 7	40
Songs Group 8	42
Music Definitions and Symbols	44
Fingering Chart	45

Lesson 1

Open Fingering 0

The open fingering is used to play the note **G** in the Middle Range. This same fingering is also used to play the note **C** in the Low Range. For this fingering you do not press down any valves on the trumpet.

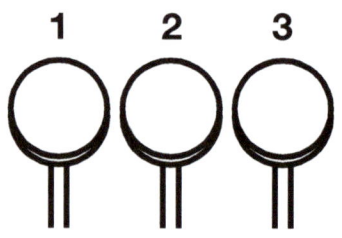  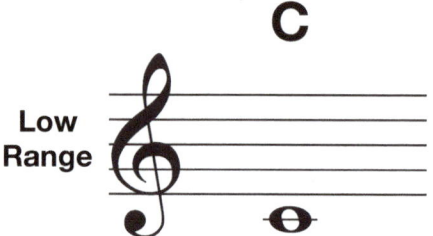

Play by Listening

Listen to the following exercises. Use the Color Fingerings to play what you hear.

1

1	2	3	4

0 ⎯⎯⎯⎯⎯⎯⎯⎯

1	2	3	4

0 ⎯⎯⎯⎯⎯⎯⎯⎯

2

1	2	3	4

0 0 0 0

1	2	3	4

0 0 0 0

3

1	2	3	4

0 0⎯0 0

1	2	3	4

0 𝄽 0 0

Brass in Color

Lesson 1

Same Fingerings/Different Notes

In the Color Fingerings chart below you can see how the 7 different fingerings are used to play the notes in the Middle Range. They are the same 7 fingerings you use to play the notes in the Low Range.

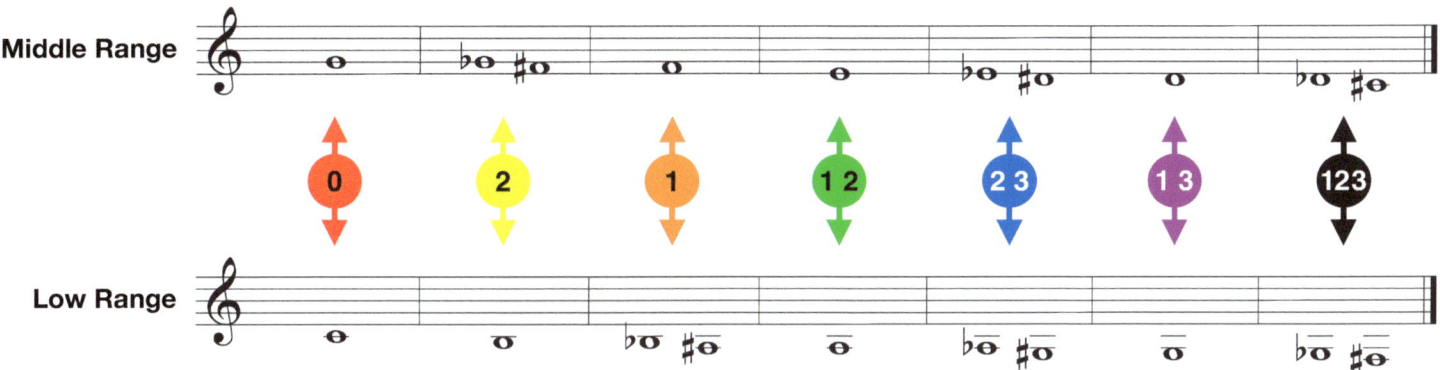

Play by Reading

Play the following exercises reading music notation.

 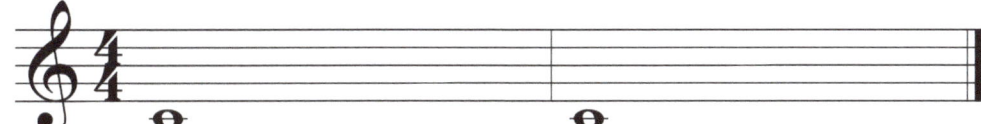

Lesson 2

2nd Valve 2

For this fingering you press down the second valve. By pressing down the second valve you make the pitch one half step lower than the open fingering. You use this fingering to play the notes **G♭/F♯** in the Middle Range and the note **B** in the Low Range.

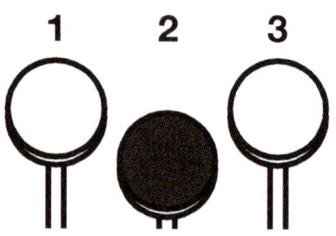

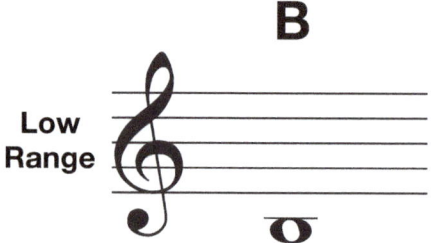

Play by Listening

Listen to the following exercises. Use the Color Fingerings to play what you hear.

4
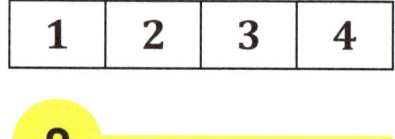
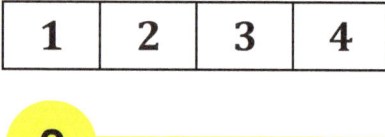

5
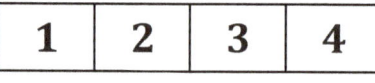
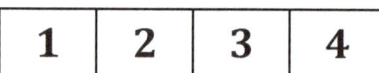

6

Brass in Color

Lesson 2

Slurs

A **slur** symbol (curved line) tells you to play two or more notes with a connected sound. To do this you play notes in the slur without tonguing each note. This symbol may appear above or below a series of notes in the music.

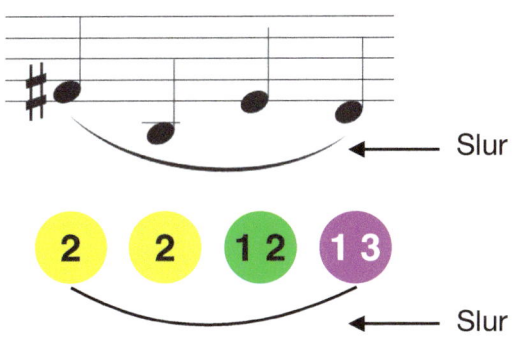

When slurring two or more notes you need to keep your air moving as you change from one note to the next note.

Play by Reading

Play the following exercises reading music notation.

 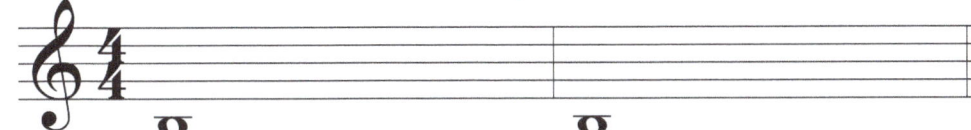

Brass in Color

Technique Exercises 1

Play by Listening

Listen to the following exercises. Use the Color Fingerings to play what you hear.

7

1	2	3	4
0 (orange)	1 3 (purple)	1 2 (green)	1 (yellow-orange)

1	2	3	4
0 (orange)	1 2 (green)	0 (orange) —

8

1	2	3	4
2 (yellow)	1 2 3 (black)	2 3 (blue)	1 2 (green)

1	2	3	4
2 (yellow)	2 3 (blue)	2 (yellow) —

9

1	2	3	4
0 (orange)	1 3 (purple)	0 (orange)	1 3 (purple)

1	2	3	4
0 (orange)	2 (yellow)	0 (orange) —

10

1	2	3	4
2 (yellow)	1 2 3 (black)	2 (yellow)	1 2 3 (black)

1	2	3	4
2 (yellow)	1 2 3 (black)	2 (yellow) —

11

1	2	3	4
2 (yellow)	1 3 (purple)	2 (yellow)	1 3 (purple)

1	2	3	4
2 (yellow)	1 3 (purple)	0 (orange) —

Brass in Color

Technique Exercises 1

Play by Reading

Play the following exercises reading music notation.

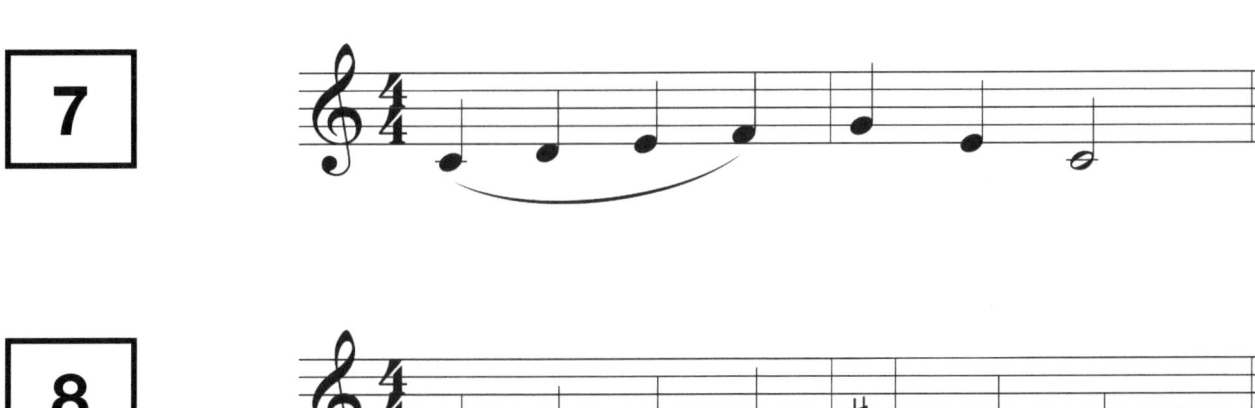

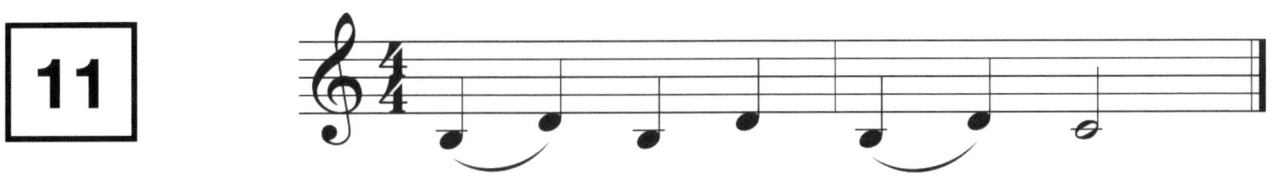

Songs Group 1

Play by Listening

Listen to the following exercises. Use the Color Fingerings to play what you hear.

12 Au Claire de la Lune

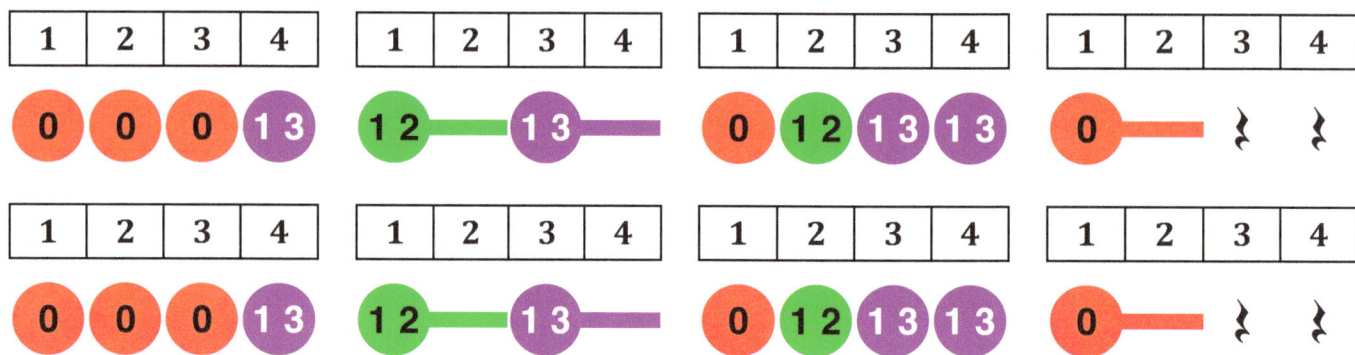

13 Mitty Matty Had a Hen

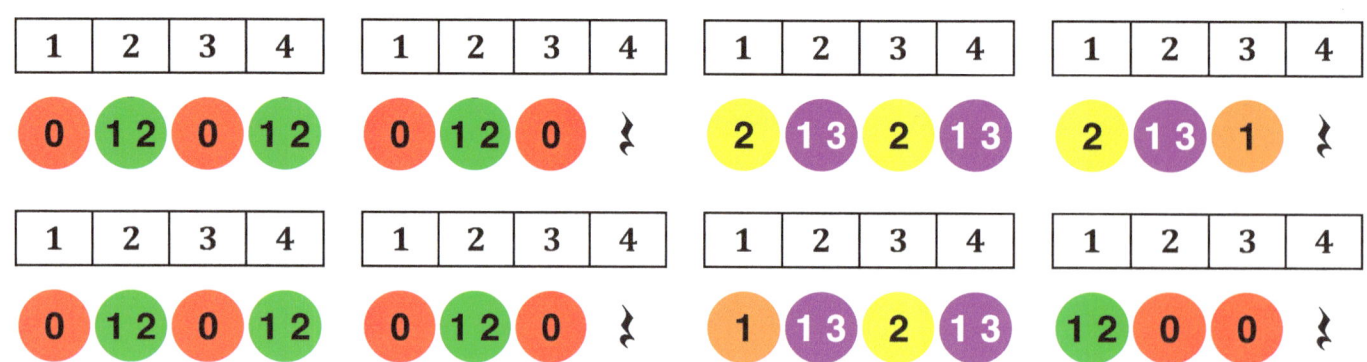

Songs Group 1

Play by Reading

Play the following exercises reading music notation.

12 **Au Claire de la Lune**

"By the Light of the Moon"
18th Century French Folk Song

13 **Mitty Matty Had a Hen**

Irish Folk Song
and Nursery Rhyme

Songs Group 2

Play by Listening

Listen to the following exercises. Use the Color Fingerings to play what you hear.

14 **Up and Down**

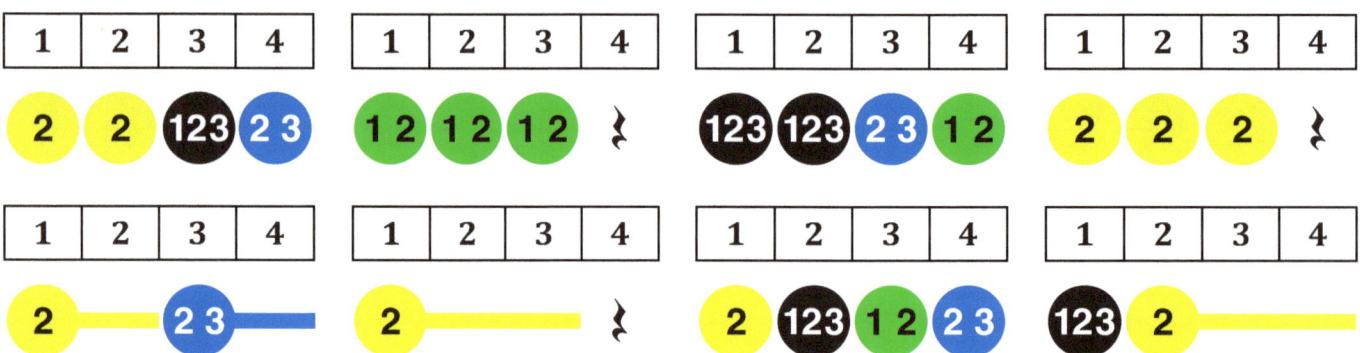

15 **Ode to Joy**

Songs Group 2

Play by Reading

Play the following exercises reading music notation.

14 **Up and Down**

15 **Ode to Joy**

Ludwig van Beethoven
Symphony No. 9, Finale

Brass in Color

Lesson 3

1st Valve

For this fingering you press down the first valve. By pressing down the first valve you make the pitch one half step lower than the second valve. You use this fingering to play the note **F** in the Middle Range and the notes **B♭/A♯** in the Low Range.

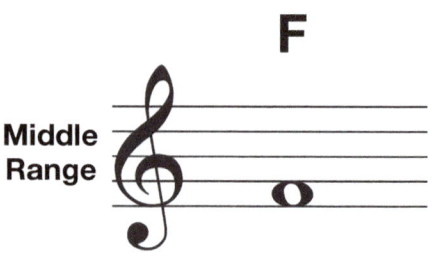

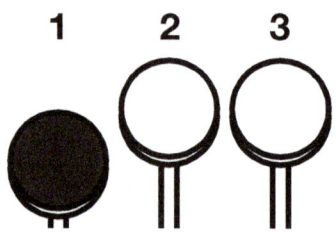

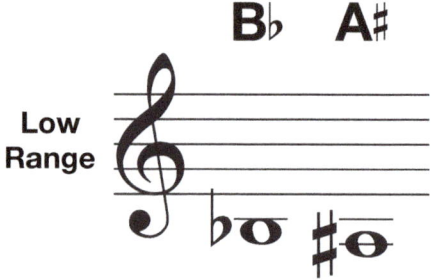

Play by Listening

Listen to the following exercises. Use the Color Fingerings to play what you hear.

16

1	2	3	4

1————

1	2	3	4

1————

17

1	2	3	4

1 1 1 1

1	2	3	4

1 1 1 1

18

1	2	3	4

1 1 1 ‽

1	2	3	4

1 1 1 ‽

Lesson 3

When you learned the notes of the Middle Range you learned that some notes sound the same, even though they are written differently in music notation. In the diagram to the right you can see how this works for notes of the Low Range.

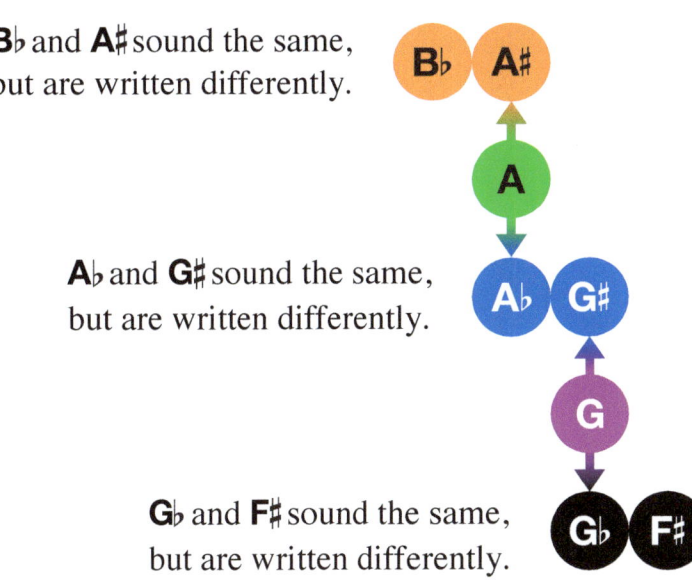

B♭ and A♯ sound the same, but are written differently.

A♭ and G♯ sound the same, but are written differently.

G♭ and F♯ sound the same, but are written differently.

Play by Reading

Play the following exercises reading music notation.

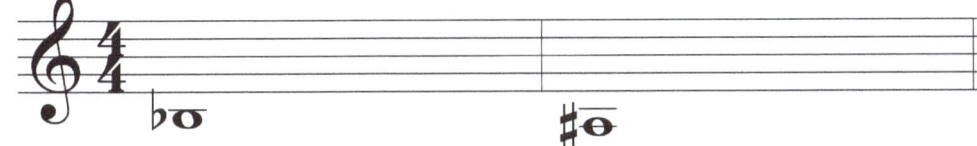

Brass in Color

Lesson 4

1st and 2nd Valves

For this fingering you press down the first and second valves. By pressing down the first and second valves you make the pitch one half step lower than the first valve. You use this fingering to play the note **E** in the Middle Range and the note **A** in the Low Range.

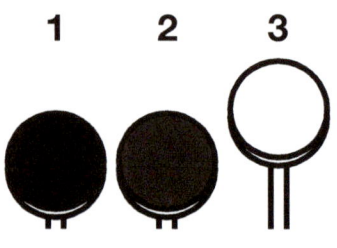  

Play by Listening

Listen to the following exercises. Use the Color Fingerings to play what you hear.

19

1	2	3	4

1	2	3	4

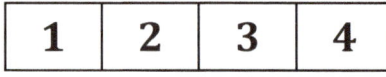

20

1	2	3	4

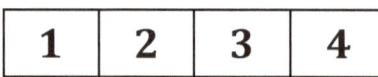

1	2	3	4

21

1	2	3	4

1	2	3	4

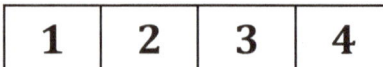

Lesson 4

Eighth Notes

A 4/4 time signature at the beginning of a piece of music means there are 4 beats to a measure and the quarter note (♩) gets one beat. In a 4/4 time signature an eighth note (♪) gets half of one beat and this means you can play two eighth notes in one beat.

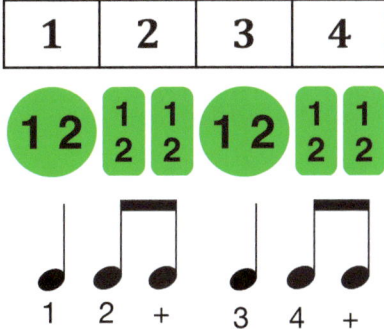

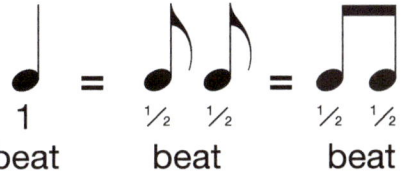

Play by Reading

Play the following exercises reading music notation.

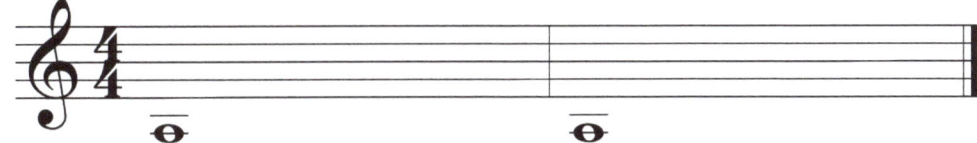

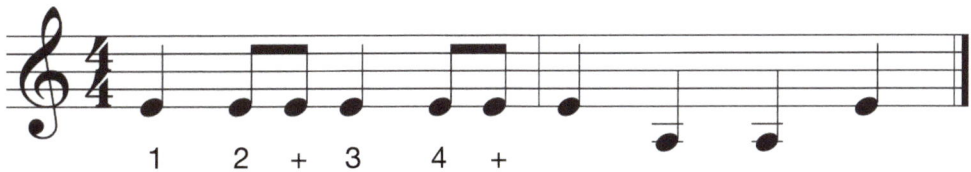

Technique Exercises 2

Play by Listening

Listen to the following exercises. Use the Color Fingerings to play what you hear.

Technique Exercises 2

Play by Reading

Play the following exercises reading music notation.

 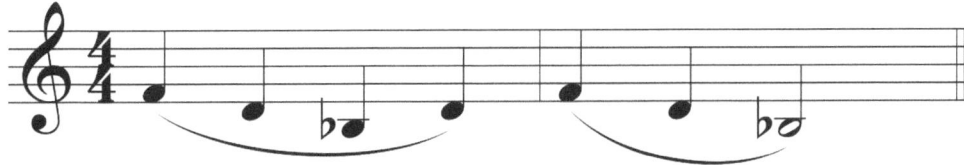

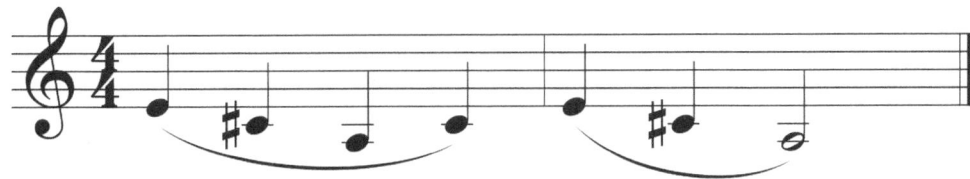

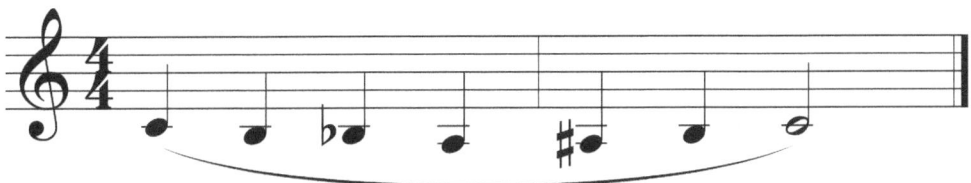

Technique Exercises 3

Play by Listening

Listen to the following exercises. Use the Color Fingerings to play what you hear.

27

1	2	3	4

0 — 123 — 0 — 1 3

1	2	3	4

0 — 2 3 — 0 — 0

28

1	2	3	4

1 2 / 2 3 — 1 2 / 2 3 — 1 2

1	2	3	4

2 3 / 1 3 — 2 3 / 1 3 — 2 3

29

1	2	3	4

1 — 0 — 1 3 — 2 3

1	2	3	4

1 — 1 — 1

30

1	2	3	4

1 2 — 2 — 123 — 1 3

1	2	3	4

1 2 — 1 2 — 1 2

31

1	2	3	4

1 3 — 2 — 1 2 — 1 3

1	2	3	4

1 3 — 2 — 1 2 — 1 3 — 123 — 1 3

Technique Exercises 3

Play by Reading

Play the following exercises reading music notation.

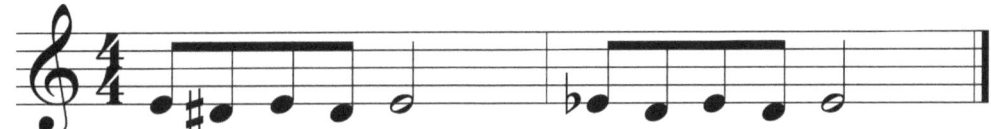

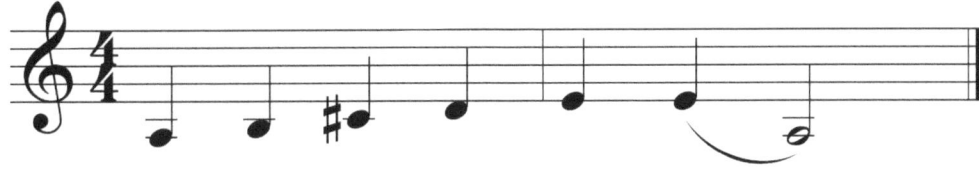

Songs Group 3

Play by Listening

Listen to the following exercises. Use the Color Fingerings to play what you hear.

32 **Half the Beat**

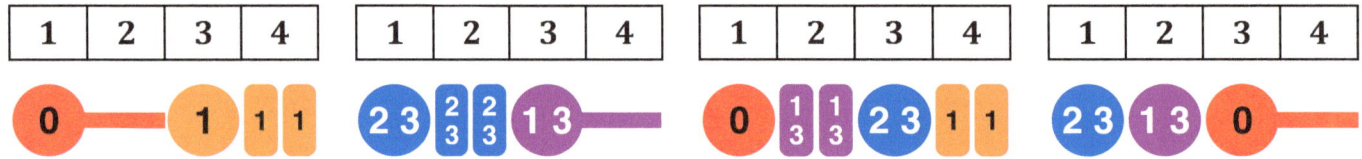

33 **Marching Along**

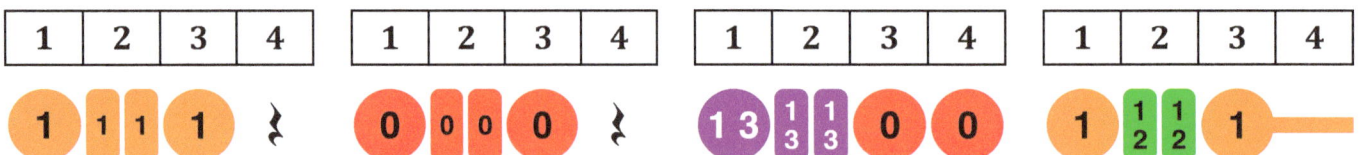

34 **Surprise Symphony**

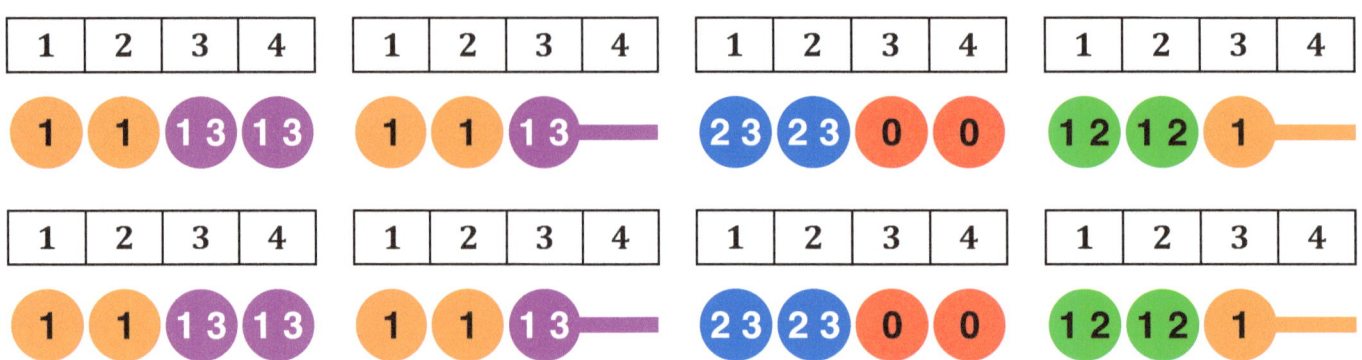

22   Brass in Color

Songs Group 3

Play by Reading

Play the following exercises reading music notation.

32 **Half the Beat**

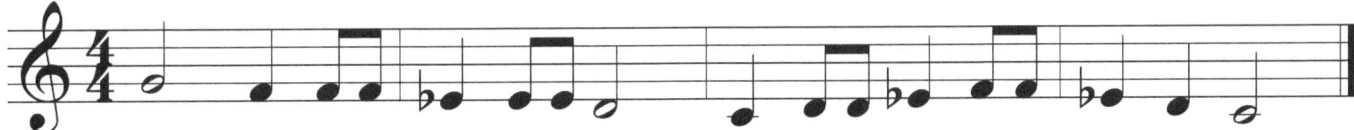

33 **Marching Along**

34 **Surprise Symphony**

Joseph Haydn
Symphony No. 94, 2nd Movement

Songs Group 4

Play by Listening

Listen to the following exercises. Use the Color Fingerings to play what you hear.

35 Mo Li Hua

36 Eighth Note Practice

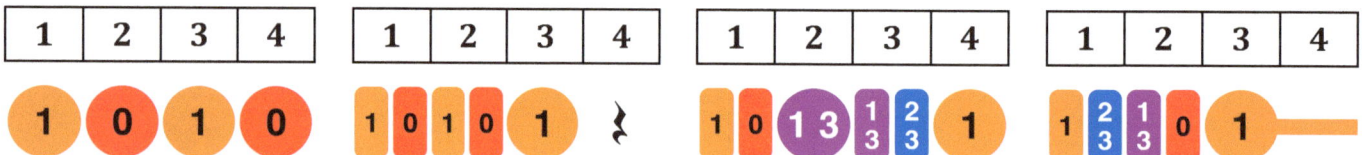

37 London Bridge

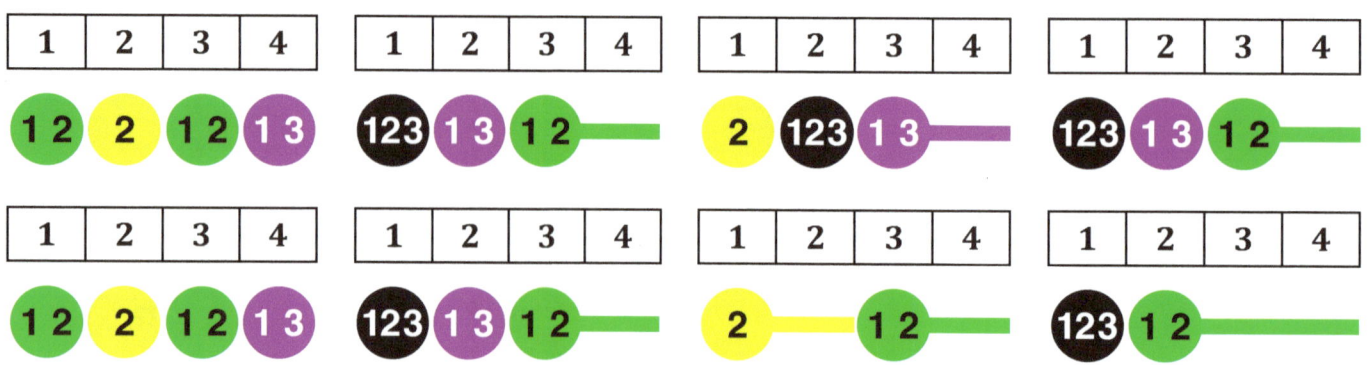

Songs Group 4

Play by Reading

Play the following exercises reading music notation.

35 **Mo Li Hua**

"Jasmine Flower"
18th Century Chinese Folk Song

36 **Eighth Note Practice**

37 **London Bridge**

English Folk Song
and Nursery Rhyme

Songs Group 5

Play by Listening

Listen to the following exercises. Use the Color Fingerings to play what you hear.

38 Johnny Get Your Haircut

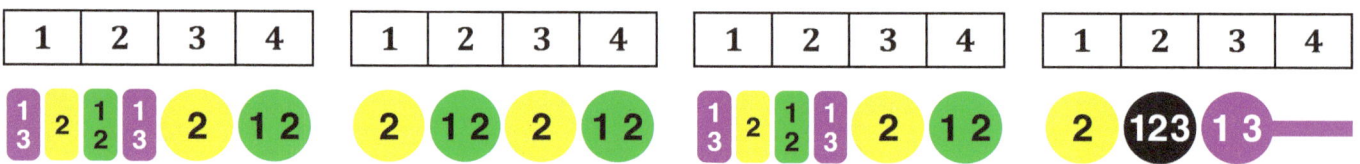

39 A Minor Tune

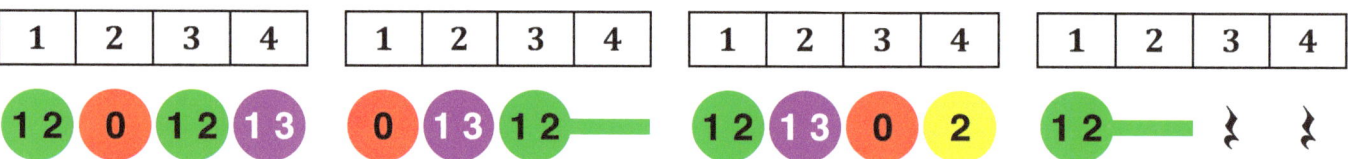

40 Arroz con Leche

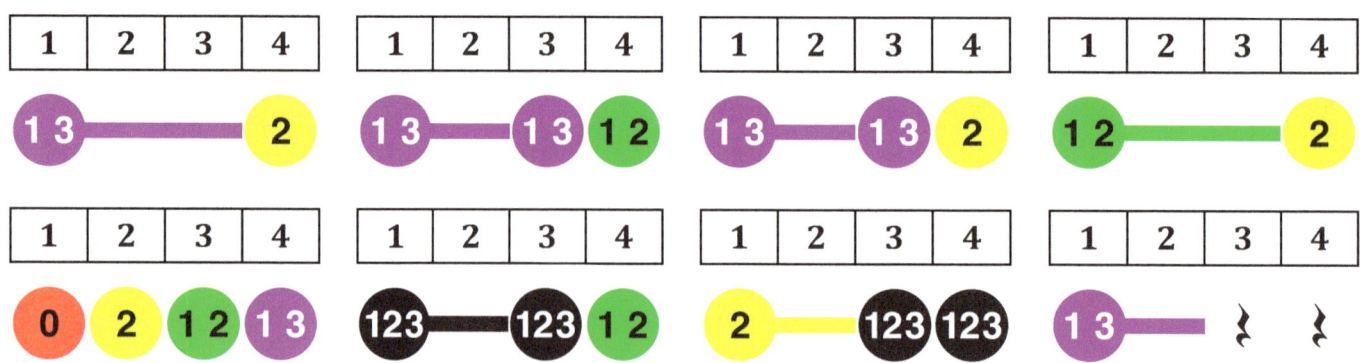

Songs Group 5

Play by Reading

Play the following exercises reading music notation.

38 | **Johnny Get Your Haircut** *American Folk Song*

39 | **A Minor Tune**

40 | **Arroz con Leche** *"Rice Pudding" Spanish and Latin American Folk Song*

Lesson 5

2nd and 3rd Valves 2 3

For this fingering you press down the second and third valves. By pressing down the second and third valves you make the pitch one half step lower than the first and second valves. You use this fingering to play the notes **E♭**/**D♯** in the Middle Range and the notes **A♭**/**G♯** in the Low Range.

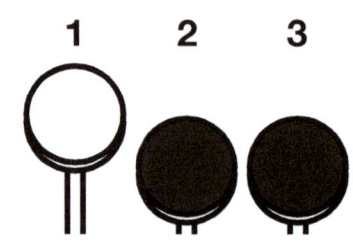

Play by Listening

Listen to the following exercises. Use the Color Fingerings to play what you hear.

41

1	2	3	4

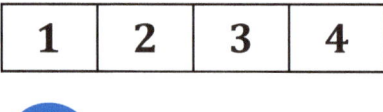

1	2	3	4

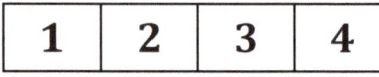

42

1	2	3	4

2 3	2 3	2 3	2 3

1	2	3	4

43

1	2	3	4

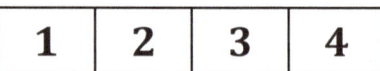

1	2	3	4

Brass in Color

Lesson 5

Building Blocks of Scales

The chart to the right shows the notes of the Low Range and the Middle Range. They are ordered (left to right) from the lowest note of the Low Range to the highest note of the Middle Range. By using the notes of the Low Range and the Middle Range you can arrange them by half steps (**H**) and whole steps (**W**) to form a scale in music. A **scale** has 8 different notes arranged in half steps and whole steps, and these notes are ordered in an ascending (going up) and descending (going down) pitch to form a scale.

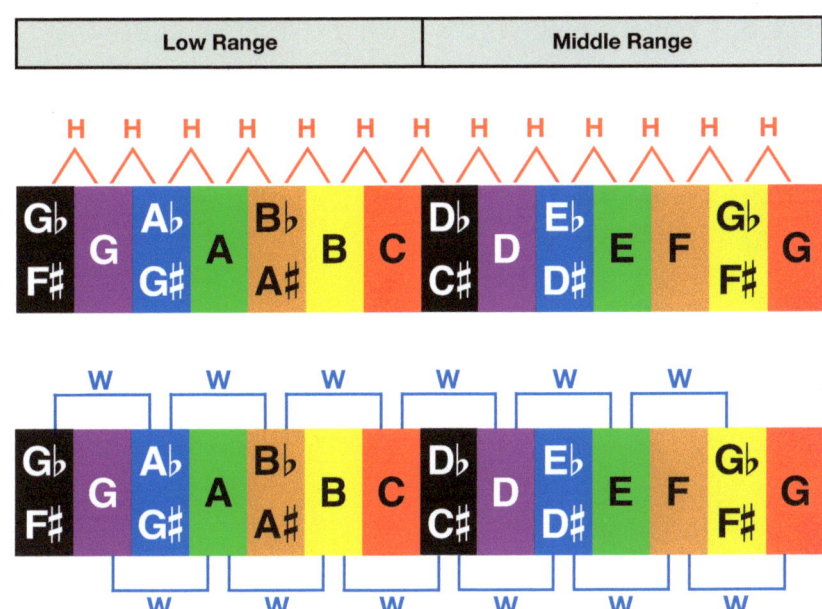

Play by Reading

Play the following exercises reading music notation.

41

42
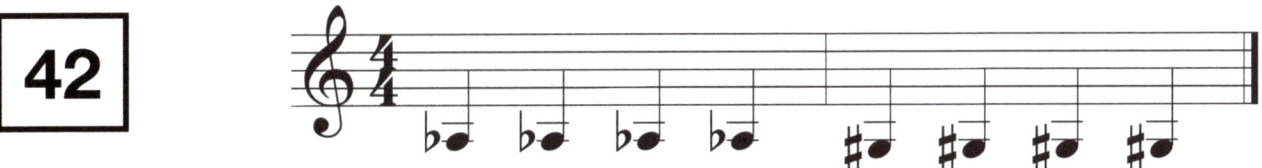

43
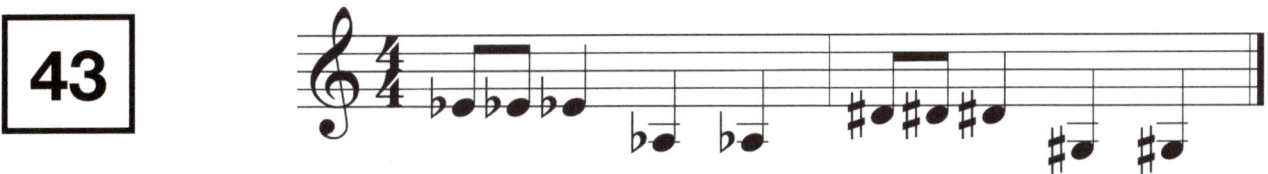

Brass in Color

Lesson 6

1st and 3rd Valves

For this fingering you press down the first and third valves. By pressing down the first and third valves you make the pitch one half step lower than the second and third valves. You use this fingering to play the note **D** in the Middle Range and the note **G** in the Low Range.

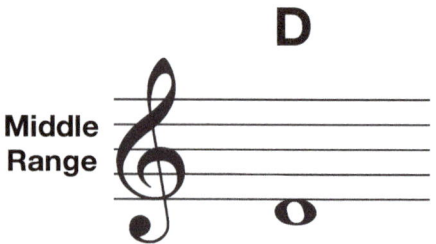

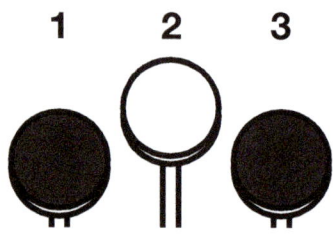

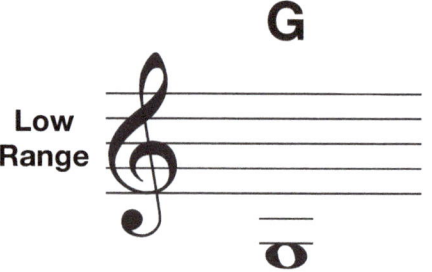

Play by Listening

Listen to the following exercises. Use the Color Fingerings to play what you hear.

44

1	2	3	4

1 3 ——————

1	2	3	4

1 3 ——————

45

1	2	3	4

1 3 1 3 1 3 1 3

1	2	3	4

1 3 1 3 1 3 1 3

46

1	2	3	4

1 3 1/3 1/3 1/3 1 3

1	2	3	4

1 3 1 3 1 3 ——

Lesson 6

Major Scale

Different combinations of half steps (H) and whole steps (W) are used to form scales. These combinations of half steps and whole steps can begin with any note to form a scale. A commonly played scale is the **major scale**. Its pattern of half steps and whole steps is: W-W-H-W-W-W-H.

G Major Scale

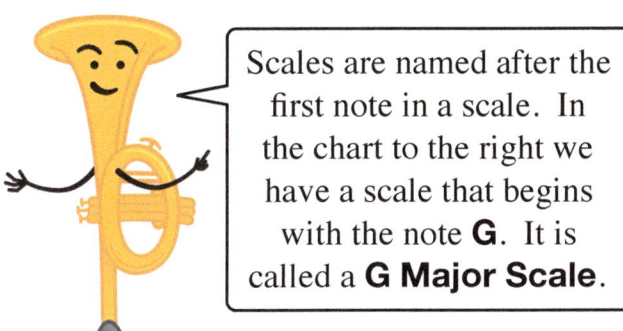
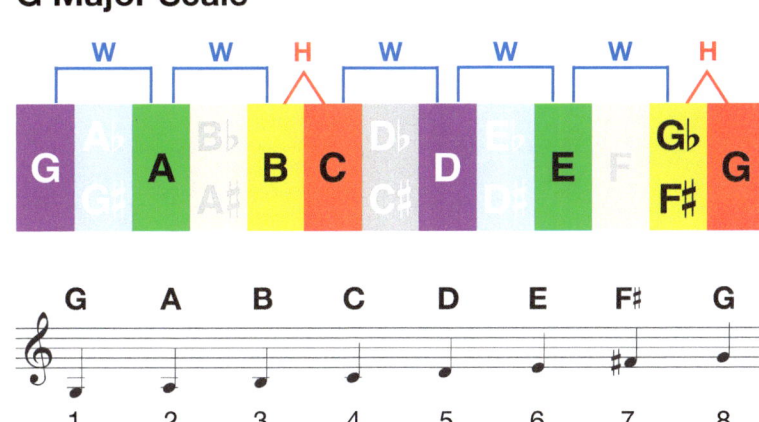

Play by Reading

Play the following exercises reading music notation.

Brass in Color

Lesson 7

1st, 2nd and 3rd Valves

For this fingering you press down all three valves. By pressing down the first, second and third valves you make the pitch one half step lower than the first and third valves. You use this fingering to play the notes **D♭/C♯** in the Middle Range and the notes **G♭/F♯** in the Low Range.

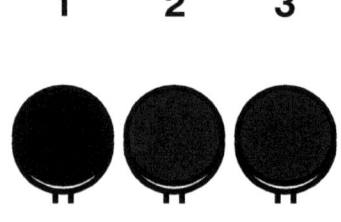

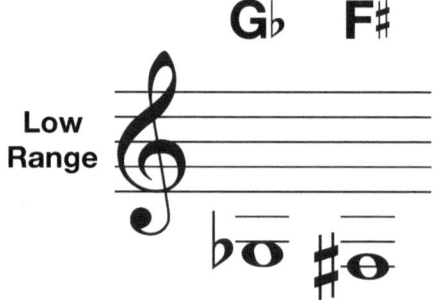

Play by Listening

Listen to the following exercises. Use the Color Fingerings to play what you hear.

47

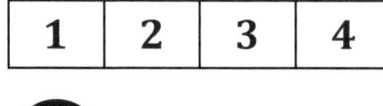
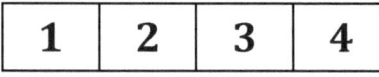

48

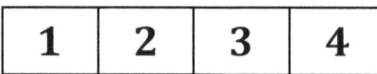
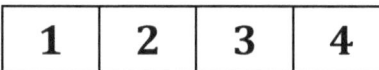

49

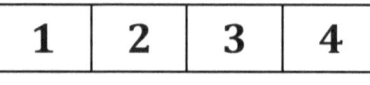

32   Brass in Color

Lesson 7

Natural Minor Scale

Different types of scales are determined by the combinations of half steps and whole steps as they relate to the notes. The difference between a major scale and a natural minor scale is the pattern of half steps and whole steps. The pattern for a **natural minor scale** is: **W-H-W-W-H-W-W**.

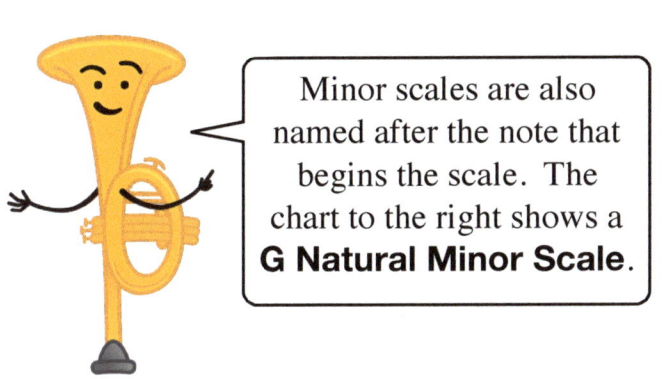

Minor scales are also named after the note that begins the scale. The chart to the right shows a **G Natural Minor Scale**.

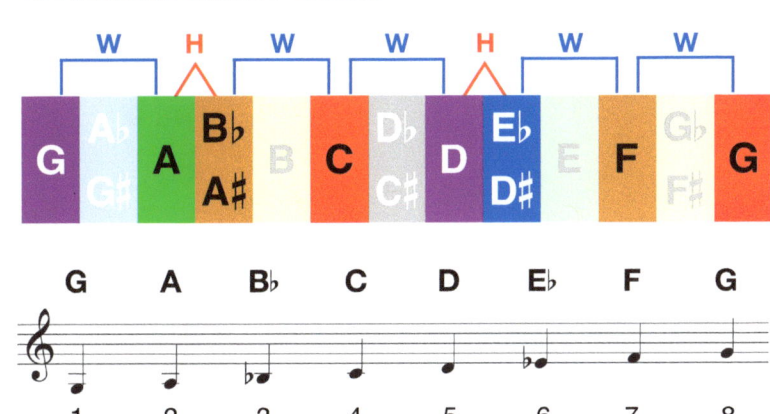

Play by Reading

Play the following exercises reading music notation.

Brass in Color

Technique Exercises 4

Play by Listening

Listen to the following exercises. Use the Color Fingerings to play what you hear.

50

1	2	3	4

(13) (12) (2) (0)

1	2	3	4

(13) (12) (2) (0)

51

1	2	3	4

(0) (13) (2) (13)

1	2	3	4

(2) (13) (0—)

52

1	2	3	4

(13) (12) (1) (0)

1	2	3	4

(13) (23) (1) (0)

53

1	2	3	4

(0) (13) (1) (13)

1	2	3	4

(1) (13) (0—)

54

1	2	3	4

(0) (23) (1) (2)

1	2	3	4

(0) (23) (0—)

Brass in Color

Technique Exercises 4

Play by Reading

Play the following exercises reading music notation.

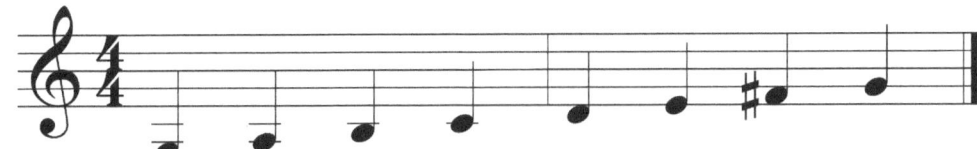

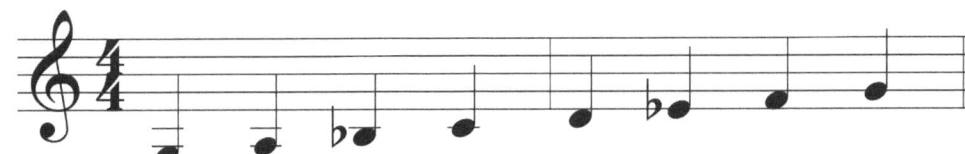

Technique Exercises 5

Play by Listening

Listen to the following exercises. Use the Color Fingerings to play what you hear.

55

1	2	3	4

(black) 123 · (blue) 2 3 · (orange) 1 · (yellow) 2

1	2	3	4

(black) 123 · (blue) 2 3 · (orange) 1 · (yellow) 2

56

1	2	3	4

(yellow) 2 · (black) 123 · (orange) 1 · (black) 123

1	2	3	4

(orange) 1 · (black) 123 · (yellow) 2 —

57

1	2	3	4

(black) 123 · (blue) 2 3 · (green) 1 2 · (yellow) 2

1	2	3	4

(black) 123 · (purple) 1 3 · (green) 1 2 · (yellow) 2

58

1	2	3	4

(yellow) 2 · (black) 123 · (green) 1 2 · (black) 123

1	2	3	4

(green) 1 2 · (black) 123 · (yellow) 2 —

59

1	2	3	4

(red) 0 · (yellow) 2 · (orange) 1 · (green) 1 2

1	2	3	4

(blue) 2 3 · (purple) 1 3 · (black) 123 —

Brass in Color

Technique Exercises 5

Play by Reading

Play the following exercises reading music notation.

Brass in Color

Songs Group 6

Play by Listening

Listen to the following exercises. Use the Color Fingerings to play what you hear.

60 G Major Study

61 Return of the Flat

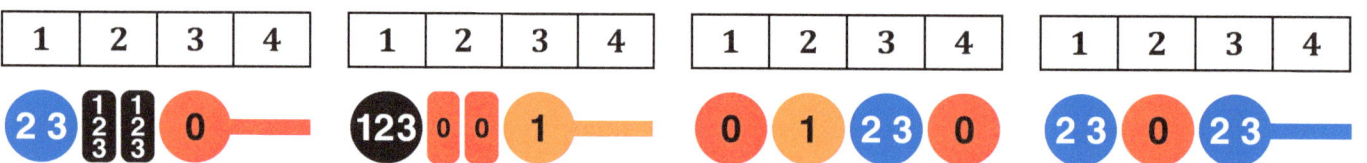

62 Walking in Half Steps

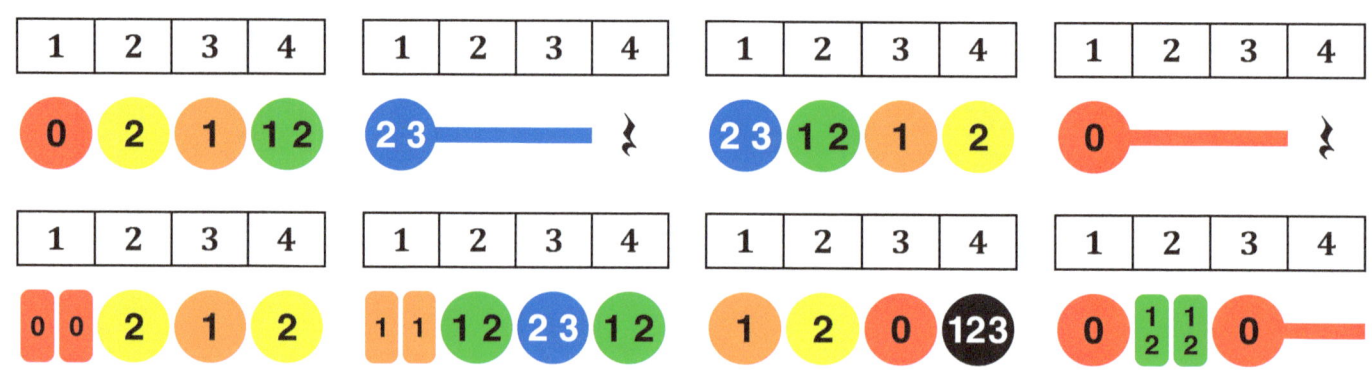

Songs Group 6

Play by Reading

Play the following exercises reading music notation.

60 **G Major Study**

61 **Return of the Flat**

62 **Walking in Half Steps**

Brass in Color   39

Songs Group 7

Play by Listening

Listen to the following exercises. Use the Color Fingerings to play what you hear.

63 Rockin' the Blues

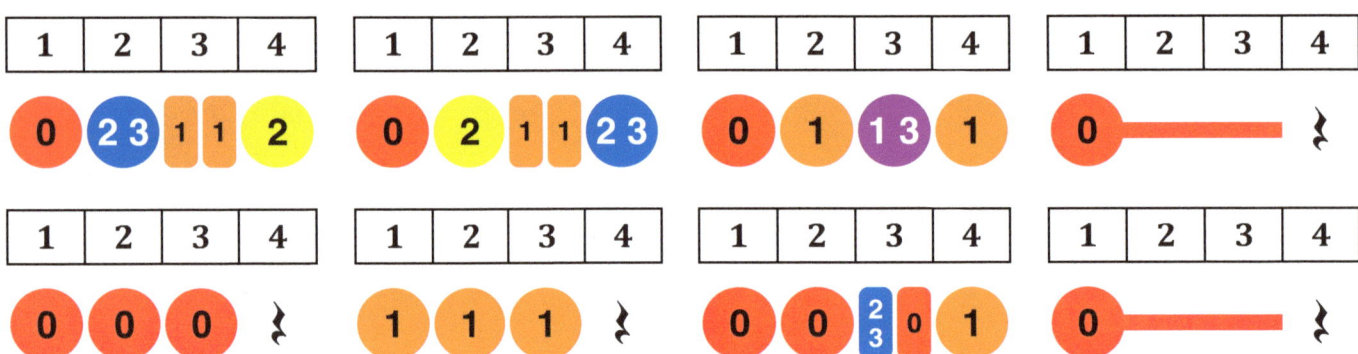

64 Yablochko

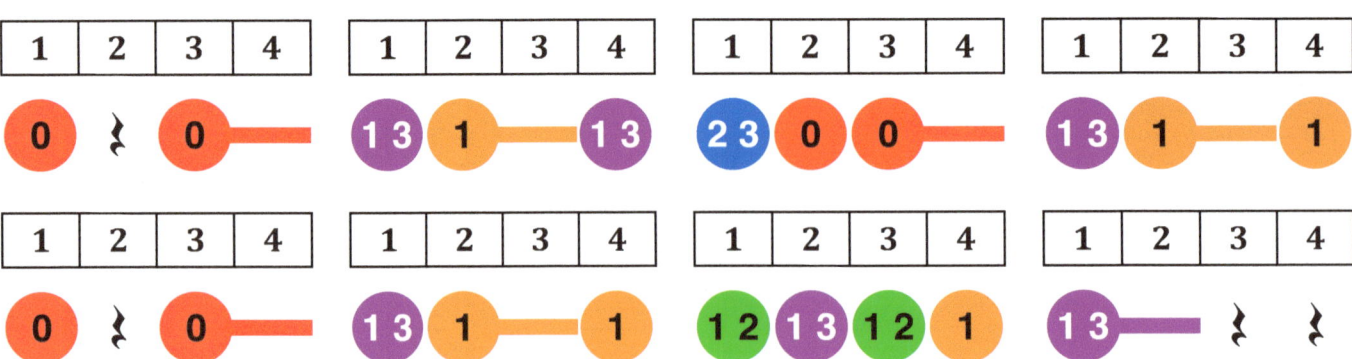

Songs Group 7

Play by Reading

Play the following exercises reading music notation.

63 **Rockin' the Blues**

64 **Yablochko**

"Little Apple"
Traditional Russian Folk Song

Songs Group 8

Play by Listening

Listen to the following exercises. Use the Color Fingerings to play what you hear.

65 Major Scale Study

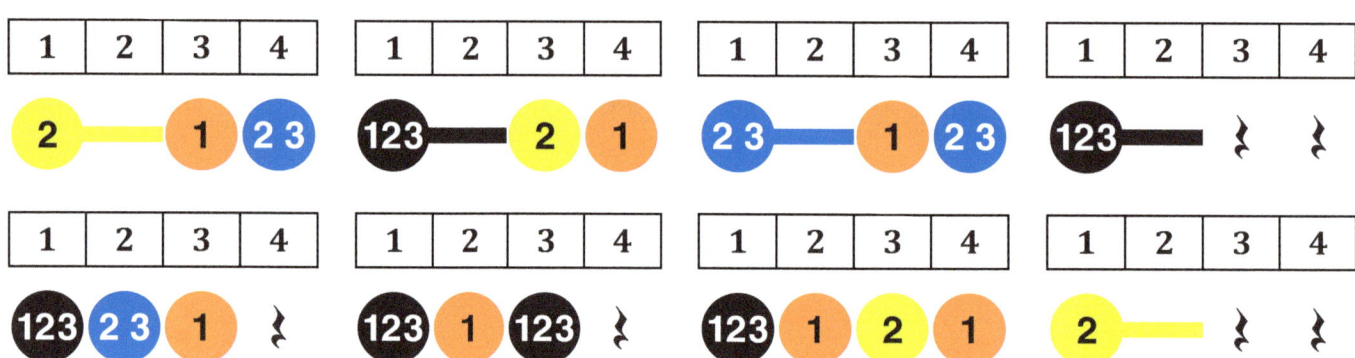

66 Minor Scale Study

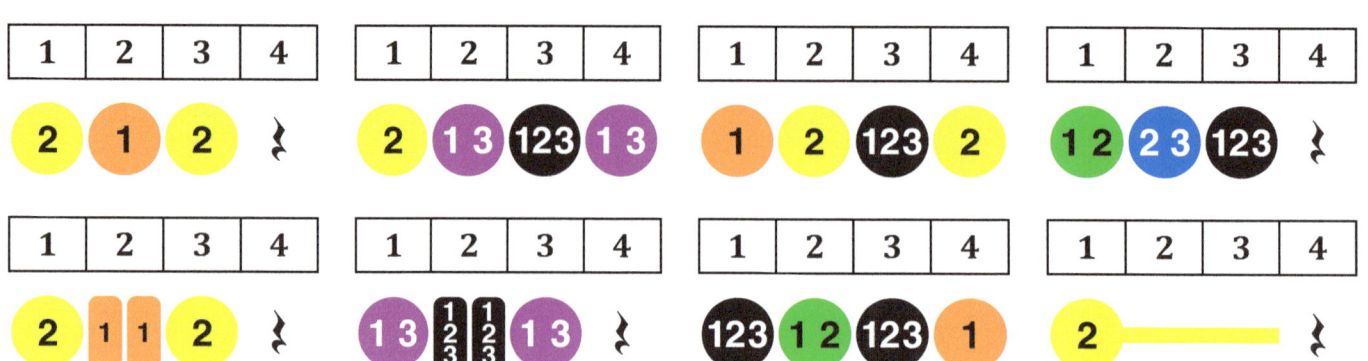

Songs Group 8

Play by Reading

Play the following exercises reading music notation.

65 | Major Scale Study

66 | Minor Scale Study

Music Definitions and Symbols

Staff

Made up of 5 lines and 4 spaces. Music symbols are placed on and around the staff to indicate pitch, rhythm, dynamics and other instructions.

```
1 ─────────
2 ─────────   1 ─────────
3 ─────────   2 ─────────
4 ─────────   3 ─────────
5 ─────────   4 ─────────
```

Time Signatures

Placed at the beginning of the staff. The top number will indicate how many beats are in a measure. The bottom number will tell you which rhythm value is placed on the beat.

4/4 Four beats in a measure. Quarter note gets the beat.

2/2 Two beats in a measure. Half note gets the beat.

Clefs

Clefs are placed at the beginning of the staff to indicate which notes are placed on the lines and spaces.

 **Treble Clef** - used for instruments that play notes that sound higher like the trumpet and French horn.

 Bass Clef - used for instruments that play notes that sound lower like the trombone, euphonium and tuba.

Treble Clef Notes

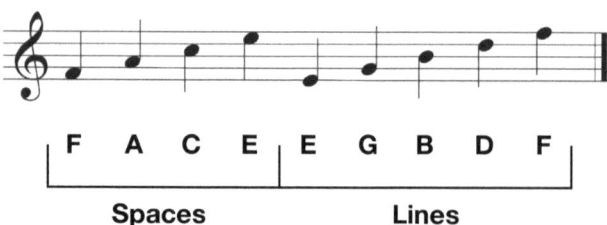

F A C E	E G B D F
Spaces	Lines

Pitch - how high or low a note sounds.

Note - the name of a pitch (Example: **G**, **F♯**, **E**).

Beat - the steady pulse in music.

Tempo - the speed of the beat (fast or slow).

Dynamics

Dynamics will tell you how loud or soft to play.

ff **Fortissimo** - very loud

f   **Forte** - loud

mf **Mezzo Forte** - half loud

mp **Mezzo Piano** - half soft

p   **Piano** - soft

pp **Pianissimo** - very soft

Accidentals

♭ **Flat** - lowers the note one half step.

♯ **Sharp** - raises the note one half step.

♮ **Natural** - cancels sharps and flats in a measure.

Rhythms

♪ **Eighth Note**   = 1/2 beat

♩ **Quarter Note**   = 1 beat

♩. **Dotted Quarter Note** = 1 1/2 beats

𝅗𝅥 **Half Note**   = 2 beats

𝅗𝅥. **Dotted Half Note**   = 3 beats

o **Whole Note**   = 4 beats

Fingering Chart

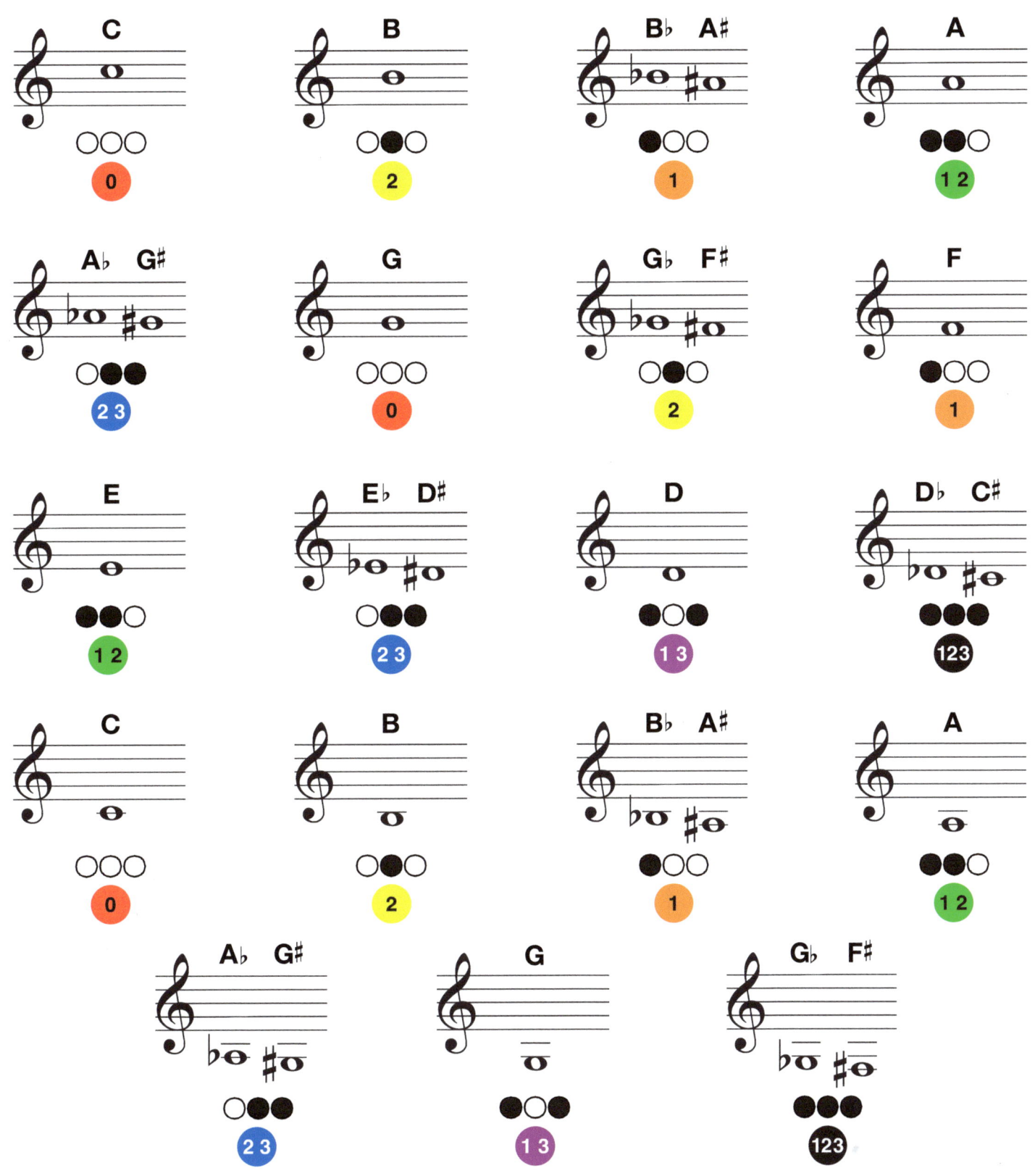

Brass in Color

Books

TRUMPET BOOK ONE will introduce notes of the Middle Range. Students will learn the basics of playing the trumpet and introductory music concepts.

TRUMPET BOOK TWO will introduce notes of the Low Range. Students will learn about slurs, eighth notes and scales.

TRUMPET BOOK THREE will introduce notes of the High Range. Students will learn about 3/4 time, dotted quarter notes, the harmonic minor scale and etudes.

www.ingramcontent.com/pod-product-compliance
Lightning Source LLC
Chambersburg PA
CBHW041117070526
44584CB00002B/198